A Touch of Simplicity

Verses to empower and awaken your senses

Genevieve Farrell

ORIGINAL WRITING

ISBN: 978-1-907179-37-2

A CIP catalogue for this book is available from the National Library.

Published by Original Writing Ltd., Dublin, 2009.

Printed by Cahill Printers Limited, Dublin

This book is dedicated to my parents, Mavis and Mel,
who continue to encourage, support and inspire me.

Acknowledgements

I want to say a special thank you to my siblings Melanie, Zelda, Michael and Zoë and friends Ann-Marie, Colleen, Margaret, Enda, Emily, Con, John, Michelle, Catherine, Elaine, Suzanne, Claire, Michela, Assumpta and Maura for their generosity of time and precious feedback.

I owe a huge debt of gratitude to my twin sister, Olwen, for her ongoing support, advice and encouragement throughout the writing of this book.

Contents

A Touch of Simplicity

Verses to empower and awaken your senses

Simple Pleasures

Kick off your shoes and lay back in your lounger.
Sweep away your worries and consider a snooze.
Slip on your loafers and let your feet take you
on a leisurely stroll by crystal clear waters.
Savour the sound of soft, mellow music.
Sip a sweet smoothie, iced tea, you pick!
Soothe your soul in a warm, sud-filled bathtub;
your new, little haven – rub – a – dub – dub.
Lap up the laughter with friends old and new.
Care for some dancing from twelve until two?
Witness a sunrise and sunset too
- simple pleasures from me to you.

Choices

An abundance of choice makes it hard to choose.
Pink or red - oh which pair of shoes?
Navy or turquoise - a little too bright?
Black or white - does this look alright?
Purple or green for the sitting room wall?
Maybe orange or brown to tone it down?
A smart new dress or bootcut jeans?
Whatever gets worn, it's got to impress!
Dots or stripes for this season's new look?
Savoury or sweet - just what will I cook?
Cruise or safari for 2 weeks or more?
Or an enjoyable stay on a sun-drenched shore?
Sarah or Zara, Thomas or Jack?
Gravel or grass for that patch out the back?
Audi or Beamer for a comfortable drive?
Clooney or Affleck for the thrill of your life?

Smile

A mile-wide smile
spread to every corner -
from one small room
to an entire building,
from an entire building
onto a busy street,
from a busy street
into a bustling community,
from a bustling community
to a powerful nation,
from a powerful nation
to another and another.
Now watch the whole world
shed new beams of light,
raise a happier head
and with inner joy be fed.
Sweep the world with a single smile.
A second of your time – so worthwhile!

Love at First Sight

I see you over there.
You see me over here.
The meeting of our eyes says it all.
You smile at me.
I smile back.
Someone leans over to talk to you.
Oh move out of the way -
You're spoiling my view -
Someone leans over to talk to me!
Oh no, not you too!
Some polite words later, I raise my head
and there you are ... still over there, lending your ear
for there's more to be said.
A little while later, you're off to the bar.
A trip, I can tell you, that's way too far.
Out of sight but not out of mind -
a rare treasure that again I will find.
You've moved from over there
to a new spot near to here!
My heart skips a beat.
That smile again – oh, what a treat!
Edging our way closer, the feeling's much warmer.
It's now or never -
be mine forever!

Thank You

Thank you for this and thank you for that.
Thank you for these and thank you for those,
a few of which, I shall now disclose.
Thank you for tending my every need,
like feeding me thrice daily and washing at speed.
For all the warm greetings, I thank you dearly.
For all the big hugs, I thank you sincerely.
For trips here and there, day in day out.
For ensuring that I am never without.
For mopping my messes and stitching my dresses,
your freshly baked bread and those tucks into bed.
For settling squabbles with sulky siblings
and forever disfavouring our futile fibbings.
For instilling in me the courage to do
as many things as possible in this world today:
to go, to see, to try, to make,
to plan to do, in my own sweet way.

Somebody

Nobody is a nobody
for everybody is a somebody.
The day someone tells you
you're a nobody,
tell them you're a somebody.
Nobody wants to be a nobody
for everybody wants to be a somebody.
So, why not become that somebody
that everybody wants to be?

The Seasons

Spring, you're the season
of all things new.
New life, new growth
and attitudes too.
Summer, you're the season
of lots to do.
Beach strolls and park rides,
a trip to the zoo.
Autumn, you're the season
of countless hues.
It's back to school time -
children, tell me your news!
Winter, you're the season
that gives me no reason
to rise from my bed
and into darkness be led.

Why not....?

Why not dine in a different venue?
Like one that offers a more tempting menu?
Why not try a more delectable dish?
Like lamb or duck or perhaps the fish?
Why not don a different dress?
A more fitted one that costs much less?
Why not try a sunnier destination?
I hear Hawaii's a great location!
Why not start to exercise more?
Take a healthy hike or a ride on your bike!
Why not take a well-deserved rest?
And return once more, feeling your best?
Why not wear a wider smile
every little once in a while?
Why not laugh a little more?
It's better than frowning – that's for sure!
Why not lend a helping hand,
to the poor and needy?
To you it will stand.

First Day at School

Let there be fun for everyone
on this day of excitement and cheer,
as you begin your first school year.
Your teacher greets you with a smile.
New friends you'll make in a little while.
You hang up your coat on your very own hook
and all around you, take a good look.
A wall of bright colours right down to the floor,
your very own seat inside the classroom door.
Within a matter of minutes,
you've gained independence.
Without any fuss, you bid farewell to your parents.
A new classmate starts a game with you.
Jigsaws, beads and shapes - there's so much to do!
New songs, new stories, nursery rhymes and more.
There's a new world waiting for you to explore.
You'll start with numbers one, two, three,
as well as letters a, b, c.
Taking in every sight and sound,
you'll mix and mingle
in your new playground.
There's so much space in this big, new place.
It's oh so cool
- your first day at school!

Chocolate .... yum, yum

A day without chocolate
is like an opportunity missed.
A tiny temptation we cannot resist.
In a house where there's chocolate,
there's always the guarantee
that with its smooth, velvety taste,
it will never go to waste.
But to be sure of a piece,
you must get there in haste.
In a delicious Dairy Crunch,
dare to indulge.
Savour each melting moment
and forget the ensuing bulge.
It's that chewy, crispy goodness
smothered in chocolate
that tempts us even more.
Out of the box and onto a plate
..... ooh I can't wait!

Don't cookies taste much better
with chocolate chips?
Think not of the load
they leave on your hips.
A combination of nuts
and creamy caramel:
a little piece of heaven
that goes down too well.
A packetful of peanuts
in their crispy chocolate shells,
a box of chocolate raisin clusters -
hmmm ... how tempting are those smells!
Have a light, fluffy choc
or a dark, rich truffle,
like a thick chunk of Thorntons
or Nestle's mint Aero.
Enjoy every bubble!

Today

It won't be long before
today becomes yesterday
and tomorrow becomes today.
If today becomes yesterday
and tomorrow becomes today,
every day gets to be today.
So, I suppose we could say
that it would make more sense
to live for today.
Instead of putting off that job
until tomorrow, why not
do it today?
Chances are it's not going
to take long anyway, and
tomorrow you'll be glad
you did it yesterday!
If you don't do it today
and leave it until tomorrow,
you may wake up in sorrow
that you didn't do it yesterday!

RELATIONSHIP

R is the respect you both have for each other.
E is the effort you make, one after another.
L is for love – love is as love does.
A is for absence – you know how it goes!
T is the time that you make for each other.
I is the interests you want to discover.
O is for openness; without it, it's hopeless.
N is for never: assume, presume, blame or shame, not ever!
S is for sharing many moments of bliss.
H is for honesty – the foundation of this.
I is the inspiration you get from each other.
P is for patience that takes you one step further.

Childhood Days

Gone are the days when the road was ours,
to walk on, to ride on in rain or hail showers.
The front door left open – a very common sight:
a rarity today. That freedom's been stolen.
A fireside story waiting to be told,
gathered round, a mix of young and old.
A rush to a roadside bush for some blackberry-picking,
then a race home to Mum for a spot of spoon-licking.
A riverside picnic on a sunny afternoon,
then stroll back home – an hour too soon!
The Sunday roast: a valued tradition,
a little less common in the world we now live in.

Sounds Abound

Coins clinking in an overcoat pocket.
Sparks a sparking from an overloaded socket.
Coal a crackling in a roaring fire.
Flags a flapping on a towering spire.
Keys a clattering on a person's hip.
Corks a popping before that first sip.
Beer barrels rolling down a hill.
Bubbling Bolinger trying not to spill.
Crows a cawing on a chimney top.
Engines a screeching at the next stop.
Waves a crashing against rough, rugged rocks.
Boat chains a rattling down at the docks.
Sausages a sizzling on a pan so noisily.
Crinkled crisps a crunching at a late night movie.

On the move

Up to Donegal with a thousand
beaches on its door.
Down to Inchadonny to explore a
whole lot more.
Over to Rosslare to relax
along the harbour
and back to Killarney's lakes
to soak up all their splendour.
In to Galway city to immerse
ourselves in the arts and more.
Out to the Aran Islands for
scenic views never seen before.
Across to Tullamore to sample
some drops of Dew.
Then home to my blessed birthplace
where the sun shines all day through.

Wishing

What you wish for another person,
you wish for yourself.
So, be careful what you wish for -
You may see your situation worsen.
Suppose you wish another
the very best in all they do.
Some day, my friend,
that very best will be returned to you.
Suppose you wish another
unhappiness and upset.
Then that my friend is just
what you are surely going to get.
So, here are a few words
to lay upon your shelf:
Wish for another
what you wish
for yourself.

A Decluttering Act

'Just how do I declutter?'
I hear you mutter.
Let's start with one room,
then move on to another.
A dozen black bags
you'll need in here.
In no time at all,
your view will be clear.
Label each bag with 'need'
and 'don't need'.
Fill each to the brim
at a mighty great speed.
Empty those boxes out
onto the floor,
not forgetting that shelf
and that old dusty drawer.
Remove every item of
each season's clothing.

Do it now, right now -
your wardrobe's exploding!
Take down those bags
from way up high
and to some of their contents,
let's wave goodbye.
As you sort through,
you're sure to reminisce.
Store all you'll need
and discard those you won't miss!
For all your 'don't needs'
stacked four feet high,
you can always dispose them
in a charity shop nearby.
So, how does it feel,
now you've cleared all that clutter?
'A huge weight lifted!' -
I hear you utter.

Flower Power

A red sea of poppies
screaming out at me.
A mass of moist mosses
meandering o'er to me.
A bank of blooming bluebells
bellowing out at me.
A wall of climbing creeper
crawling o'er to me.
A thousand dancing daisies
smiling up at me.

Rugby for a Reason

A massive moment in Irish sporting history
as the crowd rises from their seats.
A landslide victory for one,
for the other, a crushing defeat.
The natives don their province's shirt
and in their droves, descend on their local earth.
They watch with pride their team reach for glory
- joyfully recalled later in a grandchild story.
Their speed and agility on the pitch,
kicks and tackles not to be missed.
Great passing, great carrying, great physical stuff
- skills of which we can never get enough.
The nation soars to salute its heroes:
the backs and half-backs, centres, front and second rows.
The passion and spirit of this invincible team,
their drive and determination to fulfil a dream.
Our fearless fellows move in to attack,
with scrum-half and fly-half the heartbeat of the pack.
A sweet pass to the centre catches everyone's eye.
He surges ahead and scores a cracking try!
Self-belief and a desire to win get them there.
A few more winning tries right before our eyes
and a thunderous applause from the deafening crowd,
as they approach the podium for some well-deserved silverware.
Savage!

Because you are mine

The sun doth shine
because you are mine.
The clouds doth clear
because you are mine.
The stars doth appear
because you are mine.
The birds chirp cheerfully
because you are mine.
The flowers dance delightfully
because you are mine.
The hills spring to life
because you are mine.
The animals scamper about
because you are mine.
The people doth smile
because you are mine.

Change

Change isn't easy, that's for sure.
You're fully settled into a daily routine,
when a sudden imposter lands at your door.
Change can bring with it fear and worry,
like what if I'm too slow and
have to do everything in a hurry?
Or the fear of what lies ahead and
what gets left behind
- all those things that give us peace of mind.
Change can throw us out of our comfort zone and
send us spinning into a world of the unknown.
Change can lead to sweaty palms and panic attacks,
with loved ones telling us "relax, relax!"
But what if we decided to change
how we think about change?
To embrace it and welcome it
as a fresh new challenge?
To say "I am human. I can handle this."
To see change as an opportunity or
experience we'd not like to miss?

On a Journey

Long hours you did study.
Many shelves you did stack.
Come Graduation Day, you got your pat on the back.
Out of ripped breeches and into smart casuals,
you rapidly went from rags to riches.
You struck while the iron was hot
and fail to succeed you surely did not.
First job was a piece of cake,
bringing you autonomy, security
and a respectable amount of money
you were happy to make.
First product sold like hot cakes
and on the market you made a killing.
Ahead of the pack you soared to new heights,
always keen, ready and willing.
The day you both met, you hit the jackpot
and not long after that, you tied the knot.
As clear as day, you were over the moon
with the arrival of Junior a month too soon.
Some twenty years later and still in the pink -
pleased as punch with your lot,
at the end of the road you surely are not.
So where to from here,
holiday of a lifetime or early retirement?
What do you think?

Laughter

If you can at all,
fit a laugh into your day.
Try and see the funny side
of something one might say.
Make someone else laugh,
no matter who.
It can lift all your worries
and stresses too.
Spend time with a friend
who makes you laugh
and this will cut your
problems in half.
Let someone entertain you
with a joke or two.
Wear funny breeches -
you'll have them in stitches.
Have a giggle, a titter,
a chortle, a chuckle.
Just try not to burst
your leather belt's buckle!
Try to laugh after a knock
or a fall and you'll see
that laughter really is
the best medicine of all.

AUTUMN

A is the abundance of foliage apparent
on our hillsides and roadways.
U is the umbrage at our nights growing
longer and shorter our days.
T is the tableau of a thousand tints
and tones on our illuminated leaves.
U is the unwelcome cool evening breeze
never ceasing to ease.
M is the multitude of colour
on a tree-lined track.
N is the numerous sightings of hedgehogs
and pheasants who we hope to see make
their way back.

Somewhere Out There

It may not be today,
it may not be tomorrow,
but some day soon
you'll enter my world
and cast away all sorrow.
We'll know when we know,
for in a tiny flashing moment
our souls shall connect
and warmly united,
onward we shall go.
The conversation's flowing,
our faces both a glowing.
Feeling happy in this place.
How natural is the pace.
Soothing each other's senses,
we've broken down all defences.
No need for us to wonder
if we could be torn assunder.
Getting on a treat and
making each other laugh.
That's how I see myself
with you, my other half.
I know you're out there,
my breath of fresh air.
Out of the blue we shall meet,
some day, somewhere.

Time Passing

The opening seconds
of a brand New Year.
Tick tock, tick tock,
goes the kitchen clock.
As slow as they may sound
and as still as they may appear,
the hands are racing round.
The seconds become minutes,
the minutes an hour.
Before we know it, it's 7am
and it's straight into the shower.
The hours become days.
The days turn into weeks.
It won't be long till you're
on your way to climb
the nation's peaks.
The weeks become months
much too soon.
A quick glance at the calendar
- I can't believe it's June!
The months pass to
become a year.
Are you ready to be festive
and indulge in Christmas cheer?

Sandwiches

There's nothing quite like a freshly made sandwich
and an ice-cold bevy straight from the fridge.
Strips of streaky bacon or beef cold and lean,
layers of lettuce all crispy and green.
Peppers or sweetcorn to add some colour,
some salt for seasoning or perhaps some pepper?
A spoonful of mayo to bring out the best,
a squeeze of lemon to add some zest.
The freshest BLT from your local shop,
with drops of olive oil drizzled on top.
'Butter or mayo on your sandwich, Mam?'
'Neither today thanks, just coleslaw and ham.'
'Anything else I can get for you?'
'My sandwich cut in two and a large coke, thank you!'

The Magic of Music

I never say no to a musical treat.
Whatever the rhythm, tempo or pace,
I'm always ready to feel the beat.
From R & B to rock and pop,
swing and jazz to classical and dance
- once it starts, I just can't stop.
You've got Bruce, you've got Bublé,
Jackson and Sting.
A whole lot of Elvis and lots more from Bing.
A marvellous melody accompanied by
a hair-raising harmony,
singers in unison, together as one.
The flawless flow of fingers on a flute or fiddle,
with a mix of minor guitar keys somewhere in the middle.
A cascade of notes from a sweet-sounding oboe
and a polished performance on a grand piano.
Many's the time I abandon my seat
to hit the big dance floor and feel every beat.
Yeah, yeah, yeah .....
I never say no to a musical treat.

The Tough Ones

I've heard it said that
tough times don't last
but tough people do,
and with that I agree
- how about you?
They never give up
when times are rough.
They choose to keep going
and that's why they're tough.
Although they may stumble,
their world will not tumble.
They rise up and continue
to plod the day through.
They may fall once, twice
or even thrice,
but they get up and move on,
whatever the price.
They view problems as guidelines,
not red and white stop signs,
mistakes as experiences,
being burned as lessons learned.
If ever in doubt
about what they should do,
panic they won't,
for there's always a way out.

They look on the bright side
after hitting a bunker.
Negative self-talk and self-pity
just will not occur.
They believe they can
conquer, achieve and deliver,
no matter how steep the climb
- and this is what gets them there
every time.

Summertime

Oh to see a clear blue sky
and watch the jet trails way up high.
To smell the scent of freshly cut grass
and hear the haymakers as they pass.
Oh to catch some rays of sunshine
and in the sweet summer's air
be able to dine.
To hear birds chirping at the crack of dawn,
to lie out and read on a lovely lawn.
Oh to laze about in a leafy park
and ramble the roads until it gets dark.

Moving On

No longer here but with me all the same.
Your touch, your stare, your thought to care -
sweet little treasures you've taken elsewhere.
The moments shared – there were hundreds,
maybe more,
now silent memories to cherish and forever store.
You fed my soul with heavenly pleasures –
that little dance in the warm moonlit night
and those reassuring whispers telling me -
it's ok – everything's alright.
Those leisurely chats over a coffee in a random location
and the riverside walks arm in arm -
the world could not but notice your elegant charm.
We took each other to places we'd never seen
and met new, friendly faces -
you know who I mean?
My passion for life, you said, blew you away
but sadly, I say, did not tempt you to stay.
I'm sailing on a new shore and offering myself to a new one.
My door is wide open, come in and render me beholden.

Manners, Please!

Allow me to teach you
some simple etiquette -
to keep for always
and never forget.
Use 'please' and 'thank you'
throughout the day.
Articulate well, whatever you say.
Ask 'May I...?' not 'Can I...?'
when seeking permission.
Never interrupt the flow of
one's conversation.
Waste not your energy on
mouthfuls of cheek.
Kind words to others
I advise you to speak.
Choose a warm smile
to greet the nation,
in spite of your mood,
whatever the occasion.
Put others before you
when opening doors,
or pouring a drink -
the pleasure is yours!
Consider some people
you're likely to meet,
like a Mum-to-be or an OAP.

Just rise to your feet
and offer your seat.
On streets or pavements,
leave not your refuse;
with an abundance of bins out there,
you've got no excuse!
Show respect to all people, young and old.
Assist them and listen with interest
when they've a story to be told.
And last but not least,
after a yawn, cough or sneeze,
apologise at once with an
'excuse me!', please!

My Favourite Things

A clear blue sky whatever the season.
Children chuckling for no simple reason.
A baby's smile to warm the heart.
A loving couple never to part.
Ocean strides on a starlit night.
Sun-kissed beaches – oh what a sight!
Tasty treats made specially by Mum,
like a light, fluffy sponge to tickle your tum.
A bunch of pretty flowers to brighten your day.
A whirlwind romance that's here to stay.
A really good book by a cosy home fire.
A glass of good red with your heart's desire.
Musical masterpieces to fill the air.
Tales of times past - care to share?
The wholesome nurturing a family brings,
and the company of friends
– my favourite things.

Silence

The traffic passes.
Loaded lorries.
Busy buses.
Cars, cars and more cars.
Many, many motorbikes
weaving in and out.
People talking, perhaps shouting.
No idea what about.
Children playing ball.
One ordering, the rest
following.
Arms in the air in frustration.
Dogs on the loose
running up and down.
Staring out my window.
Cannot hear a sound -
Golden.

Have you ever wondered...?

Have you ever wondered why our skies are blue
and our grasses green?
Why clouds and raindrops there are never too few
and the air we breathe can't ever be seen?
Have you ever wondered why the sun is yellow
and leaves turn brown?
Why the stars stay up and never come down?
Have you ever wondered why he never appeared
or didn't call?
- it seemed so strange; you were getting on great after all!
Have you ever wondered what could've been?
Living elsewhere in a different scene.
Was it the timing or were you just not that keen?
Have you ever wondered what a movie would be like
if little or no music featured throughout?
Would that put its success in doubt?
Have you ever wondered what people would say
if all chocolate was banned starting from today?
Have you ever wondered why after a fall,
some of us stop, while others keep going?
Do some of us question too much and
do others say "we're as well off not knowing"?
Have you ever wondered what the world would be like
if smiles there were more and tears there were less?
And if, at the right times, we said 'no' instead of 'yes'?

Decisions, Decisions

'Which is better?', you may well ask.
Trying to decide can be a frustrating task!
Get up early, or stay on in bed?
Takeaway for tea, or cook instead?
White bread or brown? Milk chocolate or dark?
Red wine or white? Full milk or light?
Laugh or cry when you've been let down?
Grin and bear it, or show a big frown?
Follow your heart, or follow your head?
Stay single, or decide to get wed?
Sit and wait for them to ring,
or go ahead and do your own thing?
Settle in the country, or settle in the city?
Take a year out, or start university?
Accept the better paid job, or the more fulfilling one?
Spend or save for some holiday fun?

An Autumnal Moment

Lingering aimlessly
on a lush green carpet.
Its soft, blowing blades
tickle my feet.
Rusty red leaves
swirl all around.
The soil still soggy
not far beneath.
Mahogany chestnuts
released from up high -
shiny and bright
rest idly by.
One last look at
these soft, blowing blades.
Turning on my feet,
they wave me goodbye.

Stuck in a Queue

So I'm stuck in a queue the length of Peru,
waiting for a bus to get to you.
Although I'm inside, there's a breeze that won't hide!
My cardi's buttoned up, my coat is too.
A tea would be nice, but I'm not leaving this queue!
Changing from one leg to another,
so as not to get stiff,
I wonder about that guy across from me
and think what if ...?
Ten minutes later, the station's filling up.
I stretch out my arms and out of a woman's hand,
knock her coffee cup!
The look does kill, despite my apology
for the embarrassing spill!
Still in the same position in this overcrowded station,
I feel I'm on the road to Damascus –
where is this 7 o'clock bus?
A voice rings out on the loudspeaker:
'The 7pm bus to Cork is delayed.'
My back and legs grow increasingly weaker.
Thirsty and in need of a good feed -
if only I'd a book or magazine I could read.
Another look around before checking my ticket;
not in my pocket, oh where did I stick it?

The bus pulls in to my relief.
God, where is that ticket?
Please spare me the grief!
The passengers begin boarding.
I'm frantically searching!
My inside coat pocket, hurray I've got it!
The top of the queue is soon in my view.
Within a few minutes, I'll be on that bus,
comfortable and warm with no more fuss.
I smile at the driver as I hand him my ticket.
He suddenly pauses for a moment or two,
after which he announces:
"You're in the wrong queue!"

Your Moment

Chin up.
Head high.
The air is yours.
Breathe in.
Breathe out.
Shoulders straight.
The perfect gait.
Feet together.
Smile, smile, smile.
From ten down to one.
Your moment to be proud.
Words of weight.
Capture your crowd.

Thoughts

If thoughts become things,
let's think happy thoughts
and enjoy the happy things
each happy thought brings.
If we think about good things,
good feelings will follow.
Think about bad things,
the feelings are hollow.
The great thing about thoughts
is that we can choose what
thoughts to think.
Negative or positive – what thoughts
are you choosing?
Control your thoughts before
they control you.
Start off the day with 'I think I can...'
and end it with 'I knew I was able to...'
Some hundred thousand thoughts
we process each day;
hold on to the good ones
and keep the bad ones away.
Should a bad thought emerge,
replace it with a good one.
Do it now, this very moment ....
There you go, well done!

A Tiny Miracle

As this little life grows deep inside,
you stop and wonder about the first little smile.
A few kicks after breakfast
and a few more after dinner -
a sign, perhaps, that some day on the pitch,
you're sure to have a winner.
Colour of hair and eyes won't matter so much.
It's their state of health that counts
and their soft, gentle touch.
Arrival day at last
as your bundle of joy appears.
Fragile little fingers and a button nose,
rosy little cheeks and tiny, tiny toes -
how do you hold back the tears?

An Encounter with Water

Air-tossed wisps of water
invite me to see more.
Foamy, frothy sheets entice me
to feast my eyes
a little while longer.
Surface-bobbing bubbles
suggest I stay ashore.
Rapidly curling currents
warn me to retreat, retreat
and on safer soil, lay my feet.

Never A Dull Moment!

Get the kids up for breakfast and ready for school.
Remember to confirm Wednesday for their trip to the pool.
Drop the kids off and head for the office.
Grab a quick coffee before training your novice.
Attend a meeting at twelve to discuss future plans.
Return to your desk and into new paperwork delve.
Before leaving work, phone your friend Sommer
who's overdue a week, and contact the plumber to fix that new leak.
Pick the kids up at three and touch base with your hubby.
His car has broken down. Collect him at five thirty.
Prepare the dinner and help with homework.
Hang out the washing and report the tv going berserk.
Take the children to football. Drop in to see the cousins.
Leave a message with Mary for Julie to call.
Be in town for half past to collect you know who.
Then back for the children who are waiting for you.
Stop off at the shop to buy some goods for tea.
In the door at seven to cook for the family.
Help the kids to bed once washed and fed.
Begin that report due in on the fourth.
Bring in the washing and leave out the bins.
Make the school lunches - ham for Kate and cheese for the twins.
Wash the floors and lock all the doors.
Another long day .... time to hit the hay!

Making It

Majestic and monstrous.
This mountain
we must climb.
Rocks so big.
How steep the incline.
The risk of falling
and not recovering.
But step by step.
One at a time.
Crevice by crevice.
Rock by rock.
The effort put in.
The end in mind.
Looking forward.
The top we're sure to find.

Peoplegazing

A couple in red, looking exhausted,
would love nothing more
than to fall into bed.
A family of four
with rucksacks on their backs.
From where are they coming?
To just where are they going?
A well-groomed business group
take centre stage.
Oozing with confidence and
impressionable charm
- forty I reckon's an accurate age.
A two-year-old toddler
on his tippy tappy toes
- got lots to explore.
Grab a hold of him, quick!
He's racing out that door!
A few fashionable females
chitchatting over coffee
about the weather I think not,
but perhaps love and money.

A familiar face, one I can't place.
A friend of a friend, or the assistant at Mace?
A dignified gentleman finds a seat where he can,
opens his daily paper and articles within,
begins to scan.
A mother and daughter
devour a tempting, sticky bun.
Time for another? Maybe just one!

A Daily Necessity

The day it left,
we were somewhat bereft.
Vanished unexpectedly.
Oh where could it be?
Colourless days.
Brightness all gone.
Energy bursts gone.
No spring in our step
spurring us on.
Happy smiling faces -
without it
there are few.
It renewed us
and revived us;
a good daily dose.
What we would
give to see it
peeping through.
Oh sunshine.
Sweet sunshine.
A gentle plea to you:
come out and
make our day!

Free

Let yourself loose.
Let yourself go.
A lovely release.
I know it so.
No limits.
No bounds.
Unchained, untrapped
in this infinite space.
Like a bird
soaring to a
brand new height.
A colourful kite
on its maiden flight.
A liberating skydive.
A parachute parading
the open skies.
A hot-air balloon -
see how it flies.
Escape from it all.
Explore new sights
and learn new things.
Ready, steady.
Off you go.

Beliefs

Life's law,
that of belief.
What we hold true,
each entire day.
Believe in what you will:
all things good, bad,
happy, sad,
about the world,
about yourself -
your choice.
One marvellous idea,
a powerful institution,
family, friends,
success, failure,
blame, misery,
one person.
To you beliefs so limiting:
can't do it, not good enough
- from holding you, let's refrain.
To you beliefs so expanding:
can do it, well able to
- we embrace you completely.
Seep into our subconscious
and forever remain.

How long ....

How long a second is
depends on the dessert
you're biting into,
like strawberry cheesecake
or tiramisu.
How long a minute is
depends on whether you're
inside or outside the bathroom.
How long an hour is
depends on whether you're
the bride or the groom.
How long a day is
depends on how late you
were out the night before.
How long a week is
depends on the number of visitors
arriving at your door.
How long a month is
depends on the company you're
keeping on a faraway trek.
How long a year is
depends on whether the job you're
doing is fun or leaving you a wreck.

Another Chance

On my way to Rome far away from home.
A very full flight, all strapped in tight.
I put down my book after chapter three
and the person on my right starts to talk to me.
Visiting a friend he's not seen in years,
how happy and excited he appears.
Grew up together in a small, quiet town.
Played rugby and football – would never let you down.
"First trip to Rome?", I ask, to which he replies:
"Yes, and for you too?"
"No, been twice already; I'm visiting a friend,
the same as you."
The captain announces our ETA
and the weather forecast for the rest of the day.
We finally touch down and after bidding farewell,
I make my way to my central hotel.
I stroll the streets of this eternal city,
soaking up its sun and sights so pretty.
Round about eight, I don my new dress.
Then it's off to my friend's party
- don't want to be late.

"Happy birthday my friend, great to see you again!"
I ask him to introduce me to his many, many friends,
to which he replies: "Well, you do know Jack who grew
up beside me; remember his Dad drove a Mercedes Benz!"
He points to this Jack dressed all in black.
Over by the window, a face I should know.
A sudden jump! My heart goes thump, thump!
That person on my right on that very full flight.
Long-haired Jack who over a decade ago
on a fine summer's day I let slip away!

Excuses, Excuses!

‘What has you so late?
We were meant to meet at eight!’
‘My friend asked me into town,
I couldn’t turn him down!’
‘Why didn’t you join us on Friday night?’
‘I’d nothing suitable to wear
and my jeans were too tight!’
‘So was there any milk left in the shop?’
‘I found no parking space
and there was no way I could stop!’
‘May I see your ticket please?’
‘I can’t seem to find it -
I think I lost it on the quays!’
‘Are you not going for a walk today?’
‘No – weather’s much too cold and
it’s raining anyway!’
‘Can I tempt you with our new
make-up and beauty kit?’
‘Oh it’s really, really nice
but I’ve forgotten my wallet!’
‘Would you care for some homemade apple strudel?’

‘Thank you, but I couldn’t possibly
for I’m simply much too full!’
‘How about I treat you to a soda and lime?’
‘That would be lovely, but I’m so busy right now,
I just haven’t got the time!’
‘How did you get on with today’s springcleaning?’
‘Would you believe it, I haven’t started yet.
The girls called over and they’ve been here all evening!’

We Can

I can, you know,
You know I can,
like everyone can.
If he can and she can,
then you can and I can.
Now we know we can,
let's show how we can,
every woman, child and man.

Raindrops

Drip, drop, drip, drop,
on every pane and chimney top,
grimy gutter and window sill.
Drip, drop, please stop!
Plip, plop, plip, plop,
a lot less sleep for some tonight.
You trickle down, wake up the town.
When will we hear you stop?
Drip, drop, drip, drop,
the clothes, the clothes
- completely forgot!
Plip, plop, plip, plop,
still no sign of you to stop.
Drip, drop, drip, drop,
tossing and turning,
for peace a yearning.
Are you ever going to stop?

Imperfections

A powerful rock,
standing tall.
Misshapen and rugged,
it conquers all.
A natural beauty
which again may fall.
Unchosen blemishes -
it has a few.
Some long-winding cracks
to let the light shine through.
It shelters and protects
Nature's creatures
- a powerful rock,
standing tall.

Nocturnal Sounds

Howling wind against
a window pane.
Heavy drops of
pouring rain.
A distant vehicle.
A screaming jet.
A neighbour's voice,
scolding his pet.
A car door closing.
A door key turning.
An engine humming.
A freight train coming.
A baby sleeping.
A car horn beeping.
A bedroom door creaking.
A mouse a squeaking.
A hooting owl.
A screeching bat.
A knock on a door
- rat – a – tat – tat.

How can we ...?

If we don't have a destination,
how can we possibly know
where we are going?
If we lack inspiration,
how can we possibly know
what it is we want to do?
If we lack imagination,
how can we possibly know
how to create something new?
If we lack expectation,
how can we possibly know
what to expect?
If we lack organisation,
how can we possibly know
where everything is?
If we lack motivation,
how we can possibly know
how to achieve what we want?
If we lack communication,
how can we possibly know
what the other is thinking,
where the other is going,
what the other wants to do,
and what to expect from the other?

And now for the weather ...

What mood are you in today,
dear old Irish weather?
Will you surprise us by
dosing us with radiant sunshine?
One brilliant ray would make our day!
Or will you stick to tradition and
drench us with those
dreaded, dreary raindrops?
Will you offer us mild temperatures
so we can dress more lightly,
so our children can play in
the fresh open air,
so we can proceed with our leisure pursuits
and get to work on our outdoor chores?
Or will you turn bitterly cold
without warning,
leaving us with one desire only:
to remain under the duvet
until a more temperate morning?
Will you deliver a kind, gentle breeze,
soothing our skin and
colouring our cheeks?
Or will you destroy us with cruel gale force winds,
slapping us hard and cutting our knees?
So what can we expect from you today, dear old Irish weather?
Long sunny spells with winds abating?
Temperatures rising to seventeen or eighteen?
That would do nicely – we're patiently waiting!

Just Follow This

Say hello to hope.
Bid farewell to despair.
Remember those who matter.
Forget those who don't care.
Stand with your arms wide open.
Sit not and fear the worst may happen.
Give what you don't lack -
you'll get it back.
Open your mind to fresh, new ways.
Close it to those darker days.
Never be afraid of sudden change.
Always be ready to rearrange.
Teach yourself to survive, come what may.
Learn something new, each and every day.
Throw someone a lifeline when they really need it.
Catch good advice and make sure that you heed it.

Homebound

The jet plane screams
into the midnight sky
- a tear or two
drops from the eye.
To a city of life
and realised dreams -
goodbye.
On I must move
to tackle new things.
Some soft native accents
catch my ear -
gentle reassurance that
all will be grand,
nothing to fear.
Baggage in hand,
eyes and ears wide open
to discover what's new
since I departed this land.
New leaders and singers,
radio stations and technologies abound.
New emergent thinkers
awash with ideas,
the Isle over to be found.

Livestock grazing on fresh,
green pastures.
Life so still and unchangeable
down each quiet, little lane.
Sod-burning smells
waft in the silent air.
Heavenly home cooking
eagerly awaits.
Happy to be almost there.
Homebound.

A Recipe for Success

Sign your name and cross your heart.
Today's your day for a fresh new start.
A few secret ingredients
and a method so simple.
Want to give it a go?
Just listen and follow:
Warm a little of yourself to others each day.
Add honesty and truth to everything you say.
Stir in some tenderness, affection and care.
Season with the best you can be no matter where.
Set annoyance and frustration aside to cool.
Do not let yourself crack under pressure
or break any rule.
Spoon sweetness and sincerity into your soul
and sprinkle with dreams that can all be yours.
Remove any grudges from deep within.
Drain out any mistakes made yesterday.
Open your heart and mind
and stuff them with the best that you can find.
Drizzle a generous amount of love onto
everyone's plate and serve with a smile
- it's never too late!